R.S. THOMAS
Poems to Elsi

for Francesca

R.S. THOMAS
Poems to Elsi

Edited by Damian Walford Davies

Foreword by Rowan Williams

SEREN

Seren is the book imprint of
Poetry Wales Press Ltd,
57 Nolton Street, Bridgend, Wales, CF31 3AE

www.seren-books.com
facebook.com/SerenBooks
Twitter: @SerenBooks

ISBN: 978-1-78172-111-7

A CIP record for this title is available from the British Library.

The publisher acknowledges the financial assistance of the Welsh Books Council.

Front Cover: Drawing of R.S. Thomas by Mildred 'Elsi' Eldridge,
by kind permission of the Bodelwyddan Castle Trust and the Estate
of Mildred Eldridge

Printed by TJ International, Padstow, Cornwall

Contents

FOREWORD

R.S. Thomas's first marriage has been the subject of a fair amount of rather puzzled comment over the years. His unhappy relationship with his mother has led some to think of him as fundamentally someone who found women threatening or incomprehensible; and the fact that Elsi's own career as a visual artist seems largely to have dried up after their marriage encourages the picture of a tense, frustrated and frustrating union. All this can easily obscure the role she plays in his poetry – before and after her death; and this timely collection makes us look far harder at what she meant for and to him.

As Damian Walford Davies says in his admirable introduction, R.S. was not another Thomas Hardy, making amends to a departed wife by reconstructing a relationship that in reality had failed. What emerges throughout the many decades of marriage and writing is a twofold perspective. There is, with increasing poignancy, the observation of time passing, a long shared time suddenly and alarmingly noticed: how do we put together the actual passage of years and ageing with the felt steadiness of relation, the rediscovered freshness, the silent unchanging at-homeness, neither ecstatic nor hostile? Not a particularly new poetic theme, indeed, but treated with all of R.S.'s lapidary clarity and unexpected metaphorical sharpness. And then there is something much more particular and far more painful, the awareness of an imbalance in the relationship, the sense that she is always holding back, or rather, perhaps, just holding: not conventionally 'in love', although her partner is; withdrawing graciously but inflexibly into a privacy guarded by a glass door in which the poet sees only his face; an absolutely necessary presence for the poet, and one who will not disclose whether that dependence is mutual. Read attentively, these are poems coming from an almost shocking vulnerability; think about love overflowing in "the interval of our wounding", a hauntingly ambivalent phrase from what is in fact a beautifully affirming poem.

Damian Walford Davies more than hints that understanding these poems is a necessary dimension to understanding something about the more familiar struggle with the absent/present God. Begin from dependence, the awareness of being basically helpless in an Other's hands; never stop asking whether and in what sense you are actually heard or seen; learn to cope with a silence in which often you can see only yourself, but a silence in which that knowledge of yourself comes on you like a frighteningly unsought gift. All this could be said of R.S. confronting God, but it is deeply resonant with the sensibility laid out here.

Even (especially?) for those long familiar with R.S.'s work, to have these poems collected in this way is a revelation, the discovery, almost, of a new poet in the words of one you think you know: a poet whose self-doubt is not quite the dramatised self-questioning of the great religious poems but something more pained and unsure – yet still marked by the same verbal exactness and relentless focus. This book does indeed offer a lens for re-reading the whole body of work; while in itself it is simply a testimony to an uncomfortable, often uncomforted, deeply serious and never stale love.

Rowan Williams

Introduction

R.S. and I were on the moor at Bwlch-y-Fedwen, the wind blowing across the bleached grass and grey stone, and the golden plover calling when we decided that we could live together. On the same day we found a buzzard in a gin trap on top of a pole. We were able to free it after putting a coat over its head to calm its fear. R.S. then threw the trap into the middle of the lake and the bird flew off strongly. I wonder what sort of creature the farmer thought had flown away with his trap.

Thus Mildred Elsie Eldridge (1909-91), recollecting the bleak Welsh upland setting of a marriage proposal that, in this telling at least, seems more of a practical compromise than a fervent petition – an ironic Welsh *Wuthering Heights*. An already fêted artist, trained at the Royal College of Art (and the driver of an open-top Bentley), she was the more worldly and by far the more celebrated of the two standing on the moor that day. She had been proposed to before (by another man), but had refused. The one to whom she acceded, R.S. Thomas, four years younger than herself, was then a young curate at Chirk in the north-east March of Wales, and had not yet embarked on the poetic career that would ultimately overshadow his wife's reputation. In a poem that would appear towards the end of his long life, Thomas speaks of marriage – in the thrown voice of a weary, browbeaten woman – as something 'perpetrated' (something one commits, rather than commits to, with the suggestion of a felonious act). In another poem, vows are 'contracted'. The moorland accord of the late 1930s is certainly more tender than that. Yet it occurs to the accompaniment of the plaintive, high-pitched, two-note piping of the plover (which has a dying fall). (This is the reality behind the "shower of bird-notes" that Thomas would recall in the famous late poem, 'A Marriage'.) Does that piping augur well? Painful imprisonment is part of Eldridge's remembered scene, too, in the form of the buzzard in the gin trap (with its cruel sprung jaws). And yet the two unlikely lovers deliver the bird – lovingly, one dares to imagine – and the curate hurls the snare (fiercely, passionately?) into the lake. The less than fervent event of the proposal itself (it is not clear whose gambit it was) is invested with a measure of intensity by the later act of tenderly delivering a raptor from a trap. Over fifty years later, a frail Elsi (as she was known), returning home from hospital during her last illness, would be carried over the threshold by her husband – now famously raptor-faced – in a poignant, late nuptial gesture for a wife he described as having accomplished "everything / with a bird's grace".

A number of commentators – probing journalistic biographers and the couple's son Gwydion included – have drawn attention to the gaps, spaces and silences between husband and wife. But those spaces are not to be confused with variances and rifts. A famous visual gap is that between Thomas and Thomas-née-Eldridge in their wedding photo, taken on 5 July 1940: he dog-collared, stony-faced, handsome, looking diagonally across the shot; she handsome also, and slender, her left hand clenched close to her waist. And then there are those moments in R.S. Thomas's later autobiographical writings when an undersaying or imprecision characteristically fends off proximity and intimacy – less a generational and cultural reticence than a calculated defence against the concession of self. "He became friendly with a girl who was lodging fairly close by" is how in *Neb* (No-One) he describes, in the distancing third person, his nearness to Elsi in Chirk; as Byron Rogers reveals, he was actually lodging "just across the landing" from her, in a nursery where he slept "under a mural she had painted of angels tumbling out of heaven" (divine messengers, or fallen angels-cum-devils?). It was Elsi who would later write in her journal, as a rule of thumb for marriage: "Keep your hearts together and your tents separate".

Dated the year of their marriage, a delicate sketch by Elsi shows the faces of husband and wife. The dimensions of her own face are smaller, so that Thomas's chiselled features seem closer to us, and in front of her. On the left, a candle burns with a long, blade-like flame; below, the artist has noted (of her husband's anatomy) "Ears no lobes". Her eyes have a deep wistfulness about them. She has chosen not to detail his eyes, and so, disturbingly, he gazes out unseeingly through lamplike, empty spaces. It is a deeply resonant matrimonial double portrait: the man given priority by perspective, but denied sight so as to suggest, perhaps, an incapacity fully to appreciate her achievement and 'read' her art. (Gwydion, their son, describes his father as "visually illiterate" before he met Elsi.) And yet, Thomas was later to say: "My wife is a painter. I should have been a musician so that we could have designed a church and made music in it". Though ultimately a confession of separateness, the comment expresses a yearning for a symbiotic creative relationship that was never fully realised. Always open to the demotic through wordplay, Thomas here also delicately summons the other, secular, meaning of 'making music' – and holds it at bay.

Asked, after Elsi's death, whether he missed her, Thomas replied: "I was alone when I was living with her". What too many consumers of Thomas's poetry and his life do not appreciate is that, paradoxically, such statements affirm a relationship. Admittedly, the marriage was by all accounts one of "cold hands" and "held breath" ('Golden Wedding'), in which separate spheres were preserved in unheated vicarages, where Elsi continued to produce work of remarkable imaginative power (such as the huge mural, 'The Dance of Life', greatly admired by Stanley Spencer) before she devoted her talents to commissions (book illustration, Medici Society cards) that were a good deal less ambitious. Their son recalls them touching but seldom (a hand on the shoulder, that's all). However, to call it 'passionless' would be wrong, even though it is clear that for the Thomases, married life was an exercise in cohabitation rather than a celebration of what Douglas Dunn, in his profound sequence of elegies to his wife, Lesley Balfour Dunn, calls "the coupledom of us".

Collected in this present volume is what I have chosen to call Thomas's 'poems to Elsi'. The preposition – unprepossessing and less than fulsome as it may sound – is carefully calibrated to encompass the range of enunciations here set side-by-side. These poems are 'for', 'about', 'with an eye (often obliquely) on', Elsi; some, I suggest, posit an eavesdropping Elsi and are meant to be 'overheard'. Some ventriloquise her, the poet being fully aware of the hazards of such larceny. (A significant category in Thomas's oeuvre – his poems on paintings, not included here – are all in psychologically complex ways 'poems to Elsi'.)

I have chosen not to follow an order strictly dictated by publication date or date of composition, though these necessarily shape the contours of the volume. I have also rejected a thematic rubric that would group together poems within identifiable categories (marriage, family, birthdays, anniversaries and elegies, for example). Rather, I have chosen to arrange the poems in such a way as to give a sense of the rhythms and shifting moods of married life with its patterns of intimacy, aloofness, jealousy, reconciliation, recrimination and grief. In his introduction to the *Penguin Book of Religious Verse*, Thomas himself noted that "chronological sequence can militate against effective juxtaposition". The present collection offers some sharp appositions that evoke the ways in which a long marriage is prosecuted (one might say) by two individuals who each in their own way lamented the fact that they had let another "share / in the building" of their individual identities before they had "completed" themselves ('Careers'). What the arrangement preserves is the swift development of Thomas's lyric voice, from the Georgian mode of the opening poems to the pared-down (anti-)lyric notation that has come to define his idiom.

These poems dissect the phases of a life spent "Using the same air". They anatomise spousal "concern" and "regard", and reflect on the process through which "gossamer vows" become "hard as flint". They also record the seasons of what the poet calls his "husbanding" of the wifely body, from the "rippling meadow" of her youthful flesh to that same body's "familiar prose" (what Elsi herself would later describe as her "hump-backed, gone-in-the-middle, spindle-shanked" frame). From grand Yeatsian figurings that mythologise the female ("her of the immaculate brow / My wife") to shockingly intimate details of the very moment of her death ("I recall / now the swiftness of its arrival / wrenching her lip down"), Thomas offers these poems as verbal acts that shore up love and memory against the desolations of illness (Elsi battled with ill-health for more than twenty years) and the tyranny of a world "in / servitude to time".

Traced here also is the "curvature" of a husband's tentative approaches to his wife, together with the camber of the "line of life" on ageing palms (Thomas's is a passionate, erotic even, poetry of hands). Inevitably, the poems confess the often pitiful "Conjunction the flesh / Needs". In that formulation (which follows the lines "My eyes' / Adjectives; the way that / I scan you"), Thomas deploys a pun on a part of speech, forging what one might call a grammar of sex that suggests an equation between male desire/power and his own (demonstrable) linguistic facility. And yet the poem is pitched towards the woman's "cool" response, the utter self-sufficiency of her own 'staged' artistic world – a world often characterised by Thomas as a space defended, even constituted, by baffling mirrors. Such skirmishes are played out across the full range of these poems. Those critics who see in a mother-damaged Thomas a baleful misogyny that extends to his representations (and elisions) of his wife too often fail to recognise the ways in which the poems work to expose and redress the insecurities and gaps on which male power, and its vocabularies, are based.

Tony Brown has noted that Thomas's poems to his wife draw into their orbit his other, obsessively prosecuted themes: the *deus absconditus* or absent god, the implications of scientific discovery, and a compromised Wales (whose language Elsi never learned). As already noted, the Thomases' marriage – like the poet's search for a god that became increasingly identified with a biochemical deity, as John Pikoulis has boldy put it – was in so many of its modalities characterised by silence, absence, averted eyes and suspended breath. If Thomas's deity is famously a god of the gaps, then Elsi too is a wife and woman *abscondita*, despite the fact that Thomas was "face to face / with her, at meal-times, / by the fire, even / in the ultimate intimacies of the bed". Of course, that condition was amplified by her death, so that the late elegies can be read as part of Thomas's wider theological/post-Christian contemplation of "a presence in absence". And so it would be instructive to read the late poems to Elsi not as "bursts of rock flowers amongst the overwhelming granite of the religious poetry" (as Byron Rogers sees them), but rather as granite themselves.

What Jahan Ramazani says of Thomas Hardy's great elegies of 1912-13 to his wife Emma, from whom he became estranged in life, holds true of R.S. Thomas's post-1991 'poems to Elsi': "Hardy becomes most productive of 'love poems' once he can write them as 'elegies', once death has left a 'yawning blankness' for his love to fill".

And yet the difference from Hardy (whose elegies are clearly processed by Thomas in such poems as 'The Morrow') is that Thomas does not seek to "sew up the ragged sleeve of marriage with the thread of his earliest feelings" towards the loved one, since there was no breach in their love that needed to be stitched. However, the "psychological work" and "work of mourning" accomplished by Thomas's elegies clearly share in processes of self-recrimination that mark Hardy's elegies.

All elegy is self-elegy. Which is not to say that elegy is self-serving (though it can be). Thomas realised that. And yet, in a poem to Elsi, he feels the need to write more explicitly of his own death. In the poem placed last in this collection, the speaker, having announced the death of another (figured by the lily), proclaims his own passing: "Night that has / kept its distance, / that says to the blossom / in a dark orchard / 'Open', says now / to me here 'Close'". One might say, however, that Elsi got there first. She was clearly not squeamish about death. Rogers has drawn attention to a passage in her unpublished memoirs in which she notes: "I have a drawing of my father when he died. He was always good looking with an arched nose and very very blue eyes, but not nearly as beautiful as when the ivory skin was tautly drawn over the fine bones". Rogers also records that at Manafon, Montgomeryshire – where R.S. Thomas first achieved a maturity of voice – Elsi produced a painting

> of Ronald asleep which she submitted for an exhibition at the Royal Watercolour Society. It was returned with a note saying they did not accept portraits of dead men.

In its aligning of married life with the waning of a successful metropolitan career in art, and its central paradox of intimate marital access haunted by ultimate absence, the story suggestively encapsulates the life – and the deaths – to come.

Damian Walford Davies
March 2013

THE POEMS

I never thought in this poor world to find

I never thought in this poor world to find
Another who had loved the things I love,
The wind, the trees, the cloud-swept sky above;
One who was beautiful and grave and kind,
Who struck no discord in my dreaming mind,
Content to live with silence as a cloak
About her every thought, or, if she spoke,
Her gentle voice was music on the wind.
And then about the ending of a day
In early Spring, when the soft western breezes
Had chased the melancholy clouds afar,
As up a little hill I took my way,
I found you all alone upon your knees,
Your face uplifted to the evening star.

July 5, 1940

Nought that I would give today
Would half compare
With the long-treasured riches that somewhere
In the deep heart are stored.
Cloud and the moon and mist and the whole
Hoard of frail, white-bubbling stars,
And the cool blessing,
Like moth or wind caressing,
Of the fair, fresh rain-dipped flowers;
And all the spells of the sea, and the new green
Of moss and fern and bracken
Before their youth is stricken;
The thoughts of the trees at eventide, the hush
In the dark corn at morning,
And the wish
In your own heart still but dawning –
All of these,
A soft weight on your hands,
I would give now;
And lastly myself made clean
And white as the wave-washed sand,
If I knew how.

Concession

Not that he brought flowers
Except for the eyes' blue,
Perishable ones, or that his hands,
Famed for kindness were put then
To such usage; but rather that, going
Through flowers later, she yet could feel
These he spared perhaps for my sake.

The Return

Coming home was to that:
The white house in the cool grass
Membraned with shadow, the bright stretch
Of stream that was its looking-glass;

And smoke growing above the roof
To a tall tree among whose boughs
The first stars renewed their theme
Of time and death and a man's vows.

I know fair days

I know fair days:
his lips to mine,
his child growing in me.
Selah! But fair as well

that time we lay
all night, side by side,
the moon virginal,
his sword naked between.

Questions

She should put off modesty
with her shift. Who said that?
Should one, then, put off belief
with one's collar? The girl enters
the bed, enters the man's
arms to be clasped between sheets
against the un-love that is all around.

The priest lies down alone
face to face with the darkness
that is the nothing from which nothing
comes. 'Love', he protests, 'love'
in spiritual copulation
with a non-body, hearing the echoes
dying away, languishing under the owl's curse.

What is a bed for? Is there no repose
in the small hours? No proofing of sleep's
stuff against the fretting of stars, thoughts?
Tell me, then, after the night's toil
of loving or praying, is there nothing
to do but to rise tired and be made
away with, yawning, into the day's dream?

One thing I forgot

One thing I forgot.
That I had been sent back
to live life over again
and live it better. Was there
music? I had heard it before
with insufficient attention.
Was there beauty? I had not
taken my fill of gazing.
Had I loved? What my excuse
for not loving? Need we be taught
love? The ones I betrayed,
let down, met me with different
faces, in strange clothes;
it was a test to see whether
I remembered. The call to reflection
was repeated: I was reminded
I had passed on. The same
fruit was offered me and I forgot
I had tasted it before. One
met me and I recognized her
by her patience. How, determining
to lie down, to come together
without lust, and without shame,
could we avoid the child who rose
to us out of the ruins
of the first child, guilelessly smiling
and full of the genes' malevolence as ever.

Gifts

From my father my strong heart,
My weak stomach.
From my mother the fear.

From my sad country the shame.

To my wife all I have
Saving only the love
That is not mine to give.

To my one son the hunger.

Ap Huw's Testament

There are four verses to put down
For the four people in my life,
Father, mother, wife

And the one child. Let me begin
With her of the immaculate brow
My wife; she loves me. I know how.

My mother gave me the breast's milk
Generously, but grew mean after,
Envying me my detached laughter.

My father was a passionate man,
Wrecked after leaving the sea
In her love's shallows. He grieves in me.

What shall I say of my boy,
Tall, fair? He is young yet;
Keep his feet free of the world's net.

The Untamed

My garden is the wild
  Sea of the grass. Her garden
Shelters between walls.
    The tide could break in;
    I should be sorry for this.

There is peace there of a kind,
  Though not the deep peace
Of wild places. Her care
    For green life has enabled
    The weak things to grow.

Despite my first love,
  I take sometimes her hand,
Following strait paths
    Between flowers, the nostril
    Clogged with their thick scent.

The old softness of lawns
  Persuading the slow foot
Leads to defection; the silence
    Holds with its gloved hand
    The wild hawk of the mind.

But not for long, windows,
  Opening in the trees
Call the mind back
    To its true eyrie; I stoop
    Here only in play.

Anniversary

Nineteen years now
Under the same roof
Eating our bread,
Using the same air;
Sighing, if one sighs,
Meeting the other's
Words with a look
That thaws suspicion.

Nineteen years now
Sharing life's table,
And not to be first
To call the meal long
We balance it thoughtfully
On the tip of the tongue,
Careful to maintain
The strict palate.

Nineteen years now
Keeping simple house,
Opening the door
To friend and stranger;
Opening the womb
Softly to let enter
The one child
With his huge hunger.

Touching

She kept touching me,
As a woman will
Accidentally, so the response,
When given, is
A presumption.
I retained my
Balance, letting her sway
To her cost. The lips' prose
Ticked on, regulating
Her voltage.
Such insulation!
But necessary; their flair
For some small fun with
The current being
An injustice.
It is the man burns.

All Right

I look. You look
Away. No colour,
No ruffling of the brow's
Surface betrays
Your feeling. As though I
Were not here; as
Though you were your own
Mirror, you arrange yourself
For the play. My eyes'
Adjectives; the way that
I scan you; the
Conjunction the flesh
Needs – all these
Are as nothing
To you. Serene, cool,
Motionless, no statue
Could show less
The impression of
My regard. Madam, I
Grant the artistry
Of your part. Let us
Consider it, then,
A finished performance.

Careers

Fifty-two years,
most of them taken in
growing or in the
illusion of it – what does the mem-
ory number as one's
property? The broken elbow?
the lost toy? The pain has
vanished, but the soft flesh
that suffered it is mine still.

There is a house with
a face mooning at the glass
of windows. Those eyes – I look
at not with them, but something of
their melancholy I
begin to lay claim to as my own.

A boy in school:
his lessons are
my lessons, his
punishments I learn to deserve.
I stand up in him,
tall as I am
now, but without per-
spective. Distant objects
are too distant, yet will arrive
soon. How his words
muddle me; how my deeds
betray him. That is not
our intention; but where I should
be one with him, I am one now
with another. Before I had time
to complete myself, I let her share
in the building. This that I am
now – too many

labourers. What is mine is
not mine only: her love, her
child wait for my slow
signature. Son, from the mirror
you hold to me I turn
to recriminate. That likeness
you are at work upon – it hurts.

The Way Of It

With her fingers she turns paint
into flowers, with her body
flowers into a remembrance
of herself. She is at work
always, mending the garment
of our marriage, foraging
like a bird for something
for us to eat. If there are thorns
in my life, it is she who
will press her breast to them and sing.

Her words, when she would scold,
are too sharp. She is busy
after for hours rubbing smiles
into the wounds. I saw her,
when young, and spread the panoply
of my feathers instinctively
to engage her. She was not deceived,
but accepted me as a girl
will under a thin moon
in love's absence as someone
she could build a home with
for her imagined child.

Like That

He remembers how younger,
when he was reading about love,
his love would come quietly
to his room to challenge
description, and how he would put
the book down and listen to her
version of it, with rain
falling, perhaps, and the wind loud.

Selah! It is now he who must
go, and from the familiar prose
of her body make his way back
to his book, to the memory
rather of those earlier evenings, when
too willingly he laid it aside.

Marriage

I look up; you pass.
I have to reconcile your
existence and the meaning of it
with what I read: kings and queens
and their battles
for power. You have your battle,
too. I ask myself: Have
I been on your side? Lovelier
a dead queen than a live
wife? History worships
the fact but cannot remain
neutral. Because there are no kings
worthy of you; because poets
better than I are not here
to describe you; because time
is always too short, you must go by
now without mention, as unknown
to the future as to
the past, with one man's
eyes resting on you
in the interval of his concern.

Exchange

She goes out.
I stay in.
Now we have been
So long together
There's no need
To share silence;
The old bed
Remains made
For two; spirits
Mate apart
From the sad flesh,
Growing thinner
On time's diet
Of bile and gall.

He and She

When he came in, she was there.
When she looked at him,
he smiled. There were lights
in time's wave breaking
on an eternal shore.

Seated at table –
no need for the fracture
of the room's silence: noiselessly
they conversed. Thoughts mingling
were lit up, gold
particles in the mind's stream.

Were there currents between them?
Why, when he thought darkly,
would the nerves play
at her lips' brim? What was the heart's depth?
There were fathoms in her,
too, and sometimes he crossed
them and landed and was not repulsed.

Two

So you have to think
of the bone hearth where love
was kindled, of the size
of the shadows so small a flame
threw on the world's
walls, with the heavens
over them, lighting their vaster fires
to no end. He took her hand
sometimes and felt the will to be
of the poetry he could not
write. She measured him
with her moist eye for the coat
always too big. And time,
the faceless collector
of taxes, beat on their thin
door, and they opened
to him, looking beyond
him, beyond the sediment
of his myriad demands to the
bright place, where their undaunted
spirits were already walking.

Question

Credibly in an age of doubt
advancing up to the rim
and finding oneself on the far
side, finding that the abyss
is nothing because it is nothing
but an idea. We have been victims
of vocabulary for too long.
The one hope for the future
is that our inventions will
have outstripped it. In the absence
of terms what after-life is there
for the furies? The instrument illustrates
what it is for. It is the dictionary
deceives us. Woman, whose statistics
are for the diversion of the computer,
why the sudden shambles of your face,
but that I have told you I love you?

Nuptials

Like a bird he sang,
when they were married,
on a branch of his own
prospects. Farewell, farewell
to the girls who had
refused him, celebrating
his mistake. Did she listen
to him, plaiting the basket
from which he would take
bread? Once the whole loaf:
flesh white, breasts risen
to his first kneading;
a slice after, the appetite
whetted for the more
not to be; the fast
upon fast to be broken
only in love's absence
by the crumb of a kiss.

Women blubbed for him

Women blubbed for him
and went home. A petal blown
from time's wreath, the barn owl
came drifting. In the vicarage

hard-by on the frayed
curtains, as the lights
came on, the shadow of two
faces drew near and kissed.

Remembering

Love her now
for her ecstasies,
her willingness to oblige.
There will come a time
she will show her love for you
in her cooking,
her sewing; in a bed made up
for passionless sleeping.

The wrinkles will come upon her
calm though her brow be
under time's blowing. Frost will visit
her hair's midnight and not
thaw. Her eyes that were a fine day
will cloud over
and rain down desultory
tears when, as she infers,
you are not looking. Your part then
will be to take her hand in your
hand, proving to her
that, if blind, it is not dumb.

Bravo!

Oh, I know it and don't
care. I know there is nothing in me
but cells and chromosomes
waiting to beget chromosomes
and cells. You could take me to pieces
and there would be no angel hard
by, wringing its hands over
the demolition of its temple.
I accept I'm predictable,
that of the thousands of choices
open to me the computer can calculate
the one I'll make. There is a woman
I know, who is the catalyst
of my conversions, who is
a mineral to dazzle. She will
grow old and her lovers will not
pardon her for it. I have made
her songs in the laboratory
of my understanding, explosives timed
to go off in the blandness of time's face.

The Hearth

In front of the fire
With you, the folk song
Of the wind in the chimney and the sparks'
Embroidery of the soot – eternity
Is here in this small room,
In intervals that our love
Widens; and outside
Us is time and the victims
Of time, travellers
To a new Bethlehem, statesmen
And scientists with their hands full
Of the gifts that destroy.

Sonata

Evening. The wind rising.
The gathering excitement
of the leaves, and Beethoven
on the piano, chords reverberating
in our twin being.
'What is life?'
pitifully her eyes
asked. And I who was no seer
took hold of her loth hand
and examined it and was lost
like a pure mathematician
in its solution: strokes
cancelling strokes; angles
bisected; the line of life deviating
from the line of the head; a way
that was laid down for her to walk
which was not my way.
While the music
went on and on with chromatic
insistence, passionately proclaiming
by the keys' moonlight in the darkening
drawing-room how our art is our meaning.

Pension

Love songs in old age
have an edge to them
like dry leaves. The tree
we planted shakes in the wind

of time. Our thoughts are birds
that sit in the boughs
and remember; we call
them down to the remains

of poetry. We sit
opposite one another
at table, parrying
our sharp looks with our blunt smiles.

Matrimony

I said to her what
was in my heart, she
what was not in hers.
On such shaky

foundations we built
one of love's shining
greenhouses to let fly
in with our looks.

Partner

The water is blue.
The sky over it
of pearl. Between me
and the prospect the one

who, of all others,
herself being marine-
eyed and a pearl, too,
cannot destroy it.

Acting

Being unwise enough to have married her
I never knew when she was not acting.
'I love you' she would say; I heard the audiences
Sigh. 'I hate you'; I could never be sure
They were still there. She was lovely. I
Was only the looking-glass she made up in.
I husbanded the rippling meadow
Of her body. Their eyes grazed nightly upon it.

Alone now on the brittle platform
Of herself she is playing her last rôle.
It is perfect. Never in all her career
Was she so good. And yet the curtain
Has fallen. My charmer, come out from behind
It to take the applause. Look, I am clapping too.

Seventieth Birthday

Made of tissue and H_2O,
and activated by cells
firing – Ah, heart, the legend
of your person! Did I invent
it, and is it in being still?

In the competition with other
women your victory is assured.
It is time, as Yeats said, is
the caterpillar in the cheek's rose,
the untiring witherer of your petals.

You are drifting away from
me on the whitening current of your hair.
I lean far out from the bone's bough,
knowing the hand I extend
can save nothing of you but your love.

Portrait

Speaking always with that
restraint that was itself
an excess. Smiling at us
so as to conceal tears.

Waiting so far ahead
in modesty for us to catch
up as to appear forward.
Apologising for the time

invested in her, considering
it without interest. Hostess
of life, as unable to help
herself as if she were its guest.

I look out over the timeless sea

I look out over the timeless sea
over the head of one, calendar
to time's passing, who is now open
at the last month, her hair wintry.

Am I catalyst of her mettle that,
at my approach, her grimace of pain
turns to a smile? What it is saying is:
'Over love's depths only the surface is wrinkled.'

Vespers

Listen, I have a song
to sing that time will
punish you for listening
to and you will not know it.

There was a woman
of few years and strange
name who was the apple
in my garden I reached

for and could not gather.
So I went forth into
the world seeking for
her equal, and came

back navigating by
her quick compass to learn,
looking at her, how
I was old now and she fair still.

Birthday

Come to me a moment, stand,
Ageing yet lovely still,
At my side, let me tell you that,
With the clouds massing for attack
And the wind worrying the leaves
From the branches and the blood seeping
Thin and slow through the ventricles
Of the heart, I regret less,
Looking back on the poem's
Weakness, the failure of the mind
To be clever than of the heart
To deserve you as you showed how.

Luminary

My luminary,
my morning and evening
star. My light at noon
when there is no sun
and the sky lowers. My balance
of joy in a world
that has gone off joy's
standard. Yours the face
that young I recognised
as though I had known you
of old. Come, my eyes
said, out into the morning
of a world whose dew
waits for your footprint.
Before a green altar
with the thrush for priest
I took those gossamer
vows that neither the Church
could stale nor the Machine
tarnish, that with the years
have grown hard as flint,
lighter than platinum
on our ringless fingers.

Paving

From my door to hers
the path should have been straight.
I fetched stones,
heavy as my heart,
laid them as I imagined
in a direct line.

Looking at them now
I see them bent
like the rain's bow,
part of that immense
curvature to which
all space-time must conform.

We are art's mercenaries,
firing our thought's arrows
at the mystery of things.
If love, then, be blind,
let each deviation,
as this, be as though
the blindness of the hand
were the blindness of love, too.

Countering

Then there is the clock's
commentary, the continuing
prose that is the under-current
of all poetry. We listen
to it as, on a desert island,
men do to the subdued
music of their blood in a shell.

Then take my hand that is
of the bone the island
is made of, and looking at
me say what time it is
on love's face, for we have
no business here other than
to disprove certainties the clock knows.

Evening

The archer with time
as his arrow – has he broken
his strings that the rainbow
is so quiet over our village?

Let us stand, then, in the interval
of our wounding, till the silence
turn golden and love is
a moment eternally overflowing.

Golden Wedding

Cold hands meeting,
the eyes aside –
so vows are contracted
in the tongue's absence.

Gradually
over fifty long years
of held breath
the heart has become warm.

Dying

She does not inflict
her suffering on the garden,
but is as a shadow
disclosing light is about.

In a corner, offering
herself to the sun's healing,
I found her and discoursed
upon everything but death.

'Why speak of the past,'
I enquired, 'when its reason
is in the future?' She looked
at me as does a flower,

wanting to believe
there are no clouds about,
but that the sun's setting
will be but an absence

of pain. What are small bones
for but to stretch compassion
every more finely? We left her
on her cushion of moss,

praising the garden as
an extension of herself,
as though illness could have a perfume
of its own. I remember

her eyes that were too brave
to betray her, her lashes
that wiped off her one tear
as a feather does a droplet of dew.

Her Smile

Always her eyes
unable to close
lest death should steal
up on her unawares.
Oh, not from fear, but
because she had things
to arrange: friends,
her friends, unfriendly
with one another, to be made
friendly once more; a family
to be re-assured by her
pretending she was immortal.

Seeing those small bones,
her breath a butterfly
endeavouring to escape her;
her eyes wounded
by failures of taste
never to be mentioned,
I gave my wrath rein
only to see how
it was brought up short,
trembling but becoming
quiet again under
the stroking of her infirm smile.

Two Views of a Gorilla

We confront one another,
a meeting not of minds
but of fingers. Is it sadness
I imagine on his gnarled
face, sadness for failure
to catch up; sadness rather
for what I have become,
a brother who has put him
behind bars, when all he asks
of me is that I love him?
When two such contemplate
each other, which is made monster
by the bars that are between them?

Dying, she put out a finger
in my direction; trembling
I touched it. The gorilla
postponing the death of the species
behind bars, puts out a hand, too,
which I take, putting the stars
in a frenzy. All over the night
sky their alarm rings,
warning of the danger
that, in all the emptiness
around, when two creatures
meet, they can come so close
via the emotions to meaning.

The Morrow

That day after the night death;
that night after the day's wailing,
I went out on the hill
and contemplated the lit windows
and the stars, those flocks
without a shepherd; and I asked:
'Is she up there, the woman
who was the pawn that love
offered in exchange for beauty?'

Later I was alone in my room
reading and, the door closed,
she was there, speechlessly enquiring:
Was all well? It was true
what the book said in answer
to the world's question as to where
at death does the soul go:
'There is no need under a pillarless
heaven for it to go anywhere.'

Pen Llŷn

Dafydd looked out;
I look out: five centuries
without change? The same sea breaks
on the same shore and is not
broken. The stone in Llŷn
is still there, honey-
coloured for a girl's hair
to resemble. It is time's
smile on the cliff
face at the childishness
of my surprise. Here was the marriage
of land and sea, from whose bickering
the spray rises. 'Are you there?'
I call into the dumb
past, that is close to me
as my shadow. 'Are you here?'
I whisper to the encountered
self like one coming
on the truth asleep
and fearing to disturb it.

Together

All my life
I was face to face
with her, at meal-times,
by the fire, even
in the ultimate intimacies
of the bed. You could have asked,
then, for information
about her? There was a room
apart she kept herself in,
teasing me by leading me
to its glass door, only
to confront me with
my reflection. I learned from her
even so. Walking her shore
I found things cast up
from her depths that spoke
to me of another order,
worshipper as I was
of untamed nature. She fetched
her treasures from art's
storehouse: pieces of old
lace, delicate as frost;
china from a forgotten
period; a purse more valuable
than anything it could contain.
Coming in from the fields
with my offering of flowers
I found her garden
had forestalled me in providing
civilities for my desk.
'Tell me about life,'
I would say, 'you who were
its messenger in the delivery
of our child.' Her eyes had a
fine shame, remembering her privacy

being invaded from further off than
she expected. 'Do you think
death is the end?' frivolously
I would ask her. I recall
now the swiftness of its arrival
wrenching her lip down, and how
the upper remained firm,
reticent as the bud that is
the precursor of the flower.

A Marriage

We met
under a shower
of bird-notes.
Fifty years passed,
love's moment
in a world in
servitude to time.
She was young;
I kissed with my eyes
closed and opened
them on her wrinkles.
'Come' said death,
choosing her as his
partner for
the last dance. And she,
who in life
had done everything
with a bird's grace,
opened her bill now
for the shedding
of one sigh no
heavier than a feather.

No Time

She left me. What voice
colder than the wind
out of the grave said:
'It is over'? Impalpable,
invisible, she comes
to me still, as she would
do, and I at my reading.
There is a tremor
of light, as of a bird crossing
the sun's path, and I look
up in recognition
of a presence in absence.
Not a word, not a sound,
as she goes her way,
but a scent lingering
which is that of time immolating
itself in love's fire.

In Memoriam: M.E.E.

The rock says: 'Hold hard.'
The fly ignores it.
Here, gone, the raised wings
a rainbow. She, too:
here, gone. I know when,
but where? Eckhart,
you mock me. Between no-
where and anywhere
what difference? Her name
echoes the silence
she and her brush kept.
Immortality, perhaps,
is having one's
name said over
and over? I let
the inscription do it
for me. She explored
all of the spectrum
in a fly's wing. The days,
polishing an old
lamp, summon for me
her genie. Others
will come to this stone
where, so timeless
the lichen, so delicate
its brush strokes,
it will be as though
with all windows wide
in her ashen studio
she is at work for ever.

Still

You waited with impatience
each year for the autumn migration.
It happened and was over.

Your turn then. You departed,
not southward into the burnished
and sunlit country, but out

into the dark, where there are
no poles, no accommodating
horizons. Last night, as I loitered

where your small bones had their nest,
the owl blew away from your stone cross
softly as down from a thistle-head. I wondered.

Comparisons

To all light things
I compared her; to
a snowflake, a feather.

I remember she rested
at the dance on my
arm, as a bird

on its nest lest
the eggs break, lest
she lean too heavily

on our love. Snow
melts, feathers
are blown away;

I have let
her ashes down
in me like an anchor.

For Instance

She gave me good food;
I accepted;

Sewed my clothes, buttons;
I was smart.

She warmed my bed;
Out of it my son stepped.

She was adjudged
Beautiful. I had grown

Used to it. She is dead
Now. Is it true

I loved her? That is how
I saw things. But not she.

Dusk

Night that to the stars
says 'Open', to other
flowers, to this lily
in particular, says:
'Shut'. I was in bud
once, clenched on
a thought, until day
dawned, peeled back
my petals; I was all
stamen. Love came to me
for my pollen, made
honey in a brief
comb. Was it a day,
a year? Night that has
kept its distance,
that says to the blossom
in a dark orchard
'Open', says now
to me here 'Close'.

A note on the text and List of Sources

With the exception of 'Dying' and 'One thing I forgot', which are hitherto unpublished, each poem in the present collection is taken from its original publication in volume form, as detailed in the following list.

A Marriage (66) – *Mass for Hard Times* (Bloodaxe, 1992)

Acting (48) – *H'm* (Macmillan, 1972)

All Right (29) – *H'm* (Macmillan, 1972)

Anniversary (27) – *Tares* (Hart-Davis, 1961)

Ap Huw's Testament (25) – *Poetry for Supper* (Hart-Davis, 1958)

Birthday (53) – *Ringless Fingers* (The Frangipani Press, 2002)

Bravo! (42) – *Frequencies* (Macmillan, 1978)

Careers (30) – *Not that He Brought Flowers* (Hart-Davis, 1968)

Comparisons (70) – *Residues* (Bloodaxe Books, 2002)

Concession (19) – *Not that He Brought Flowers* (Hart-Davis, 1968)

Countering (56) – *Experimenting with an Amen* (Macmillan, 1986)

Dying – (59) hitherto unpublished; archive of the R.S. Thomas Study Centre, Bangor University

Dusk (72) – *Selected Poems* (Penguin, 2004)

Evening (57) – *No Truce with the Furies* (Bloodaxe Books, 1995)

Exchange (35) – *Pietà* (Hart-Davis, 1966)

For Instance (71) – *Pietà* (Hart-Davis, 1966)

Gifts (24) – *Pietà* (Hart-Davis, 1966)

Golden Wedding (58) – *Residues* (Bloodaxe Books, 2002)

He and She (36) – *Destinations* (Celandine Press, 1985)

Her Smile (60) – *Selected Poems* (Penguin, 2004)

'I know fair days' (21) – *The Echoes Return Slow* (Macmillan, 1988)

'I look out over the timeless sea' (51) – *The Echoes Return Slow* (Macmillan, 1988)

'I never thought in this poor world to find' (17) – *R.S. Thomas: Uncollected Poems* (Bloodaxe Books, 2013)

In Memoriam: M.E.E. (68) – *Residues* (Bloodaxe Books, 2002)

July 5, 1940 (18) – *Ringless Fingers* (The Frangipani Press, 2002)

Like That (33) – *Laboratories of the Spirit* (Macmillan, 1975)

Luminary (54) – *Ringless Fingers* (The Frangipani Press, 2002)

Marriage (34) – *Laboratories of the Spirit* (Macmillan, 1975)

Matrimony (46) – *Residues* (Bloodaxe Books, 2002)

No Time (67) – *No Truce with the Furies* (Bloodaxe Books, 1995)

Nuptials (39) – *Mass for Hard Times* (Bloodaxe Books, 1992)

'One thing I forgot' (23) – hitherto unpublished; archive of the R.S. Thomas Study Centre, Bangor University

Partner (47) – *Residues* (Bloodaxe Books, 2002)

Paving (55) – *Residues* (Bloodaxe Books, 2002)

Pen Llŷn (63) – *Mass for Hard Times* (Bloodaxe, 1992)

Pension (45) – *Ringless Fingers* (The Frangipani Press, 2002)

Portrait (50) – *Mass for Hard Times* (Bloodaxe Books, 1992)

Question (38) – *Mass for Hard Times* (Bloodaxe Books, 1992)

Questions (22) – *Experimenting with an Amen* (Macmillan, 1986)

Remembering (41) – *No Truce with the Furies* (Bloodaxe Books, 1995)

Seventieth Birthday (49) – *Between Here and Now* (Macmillan, 1981)

Sonata (44) – *Later Poems* (Macmillan, 1983)

Still (69) – *No Truce with the Furies* (Bloodaxe Books, 1995)

The Morrow (62) – *No Truce with the Furies*(Bloodaxe Books, 1995)

The Hearth (43) – *H'm* (Macmillan, 1972)

The Return (20) – *Song at the Year's Turning* (Hart-Davis, 1955)

The Untamed (26) – *The Bread of Truth* (Hart-Davis, 1963)

The Way of It (32) – *The Way of It* (Coelfrith Press, 1977)

Together (64) – *Residues* (Bloodaxe Books, 2002)

Touching (28) – *Not that He Brought Flowers* (Hart-Davis, 1968)

Two (37) – *The Way of It* (Coelfrith Press, 1977)

Two Views of a Gorilla (61) – *Selected Poems* (Penguin, 2004)

Vespers (52) – *No Truce with the Furies* (Bloodaxe Books, 1995)

'Women blubbed for him' (40) – *The Echoes Return Slow* (Macmillan, 1988)

Acknowledgements

The poems in this volume appear by kind permission of Gwydion Thomas, Kunjana Thomas and Rhodri Thomas (the Estate of R.S. Thomas).

I am grateful to Jason Walford Davies and Tony Brown, Co-Directors of the R.S. Thomas Study Centre at Bangor University; to M. Wynn Thomas, the executor of R.S. Thomas's unpublished works; and to Suzanne Fairless-Aitken at Bloodaxe Books.

Thanks are also due to Robert Meyrick for his help and advice.

The Contributors

Damian Walford Davies is Rendel Professor of English at Aberystwyth University. He has written widely on the poetry of R.S. Thomas, and is the author of two collections of poetry from Seren: *Suit of Lights* (2009) and *Witch* (2012).

Rowan Williams is Master of Magdalene College, Cambridge. From 2002 to 2012, he served as the 104th Archbishop of Canterbury. A noted poet and theologian, he is also a distinguished critic of the poetry of R.S. Thomas.